SCIENCE EXPLORER

SOIL

SUPER COOL
SCIENCE
EXPERIMENTS:
SOIL

by Vicky Franchino

CHERRY LAKE PUBLISHING • ANN ARBOR, MICHIGAN

CHERRY
LAKE
Publishing

J 631.4
Franchino

Published in the United States of America by
Cherry Lake Publishing
Ann Arbor, Michigan
www.cherrylakepublishing.com

Content Editor: Robert Wolffe, EdD,
Professor of Teacher Education,
Bradley University, Peoria, Illinois

Book design and illustration: The Design Lab

Photo Credits: Cover and page 1, ©Luminis, used under license from
Shutterstock, Inc.; page 4, ©iStockphoto.com/johnnyscriv; page 8,
©Noam Armonn, used under license from Shutterstock, Inc.; page
12, ©Oldproof, used under license from Shutterstock, Inc.; page 16,
©iStockphoto.com/mdilsiz; page 20, ©Anthony Harris, used under
license from Shutterstock, Inc.; page 24, ©iStockphoto.com/joruba; page
28, ©Ted Foxx/Alamy

Library of Congress Cataloging-in-Publication Data
Franchino, Vicky.
  Super cool science experiments: soil / by Vicky Franchino.
     p. cm.—(Science explorer)
  Includes bibliographical references and index.
  ISBN-13: 978-1-60279-526-6   ISBN-10: 1-60279-526-6 (lib. bdg.)
  ISBN-13: 978-1-60279-604-1   ISBN-10: 1-60279-604-1 (pbk.)
  1. Soils—Juvenile literature. 2. Soils—Experiments—Juvenile
literature. I. Title. II. Series.
  S591.3.F73 2010
  631.4—dc22   2009002693

Cherry Lake Publishing would like to acknowledge the work
of The Partnership for 21st Century Skills. Please visit
www.21stcenturyskills.org for more information.

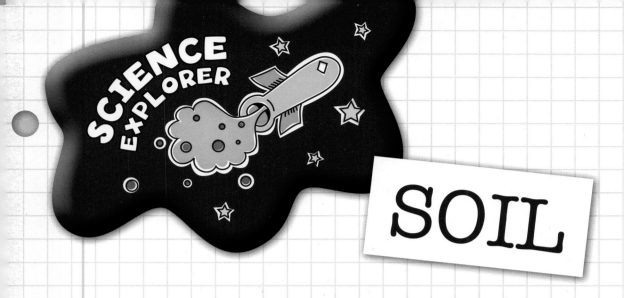

SOIL

TABLE OF CONTENTS

Dirty Science!

You'll need to get your hands dirty to learn about soil!

Do you like to play outside? Does your family grow a garden? Are there potted plants in your home? If so, then you probably have seen soil before. But have you ever taken a moment to think about it? To study it? To observe it?

Do you know that you can do science experiments with soil using things you already have at home? In this book, we'll learn how scientists think. We will use science to ask some questions about soil, and we'll do experiments to find the answers. You might be surprised to discover that "just dirt" can be pretty interesting stuff!

First Things First

Agronomists like working with soil and plants.

Scientists learn by studying nature very carefully. Some work with soil and focus on how it helps us to grow different foods. These scientists are called agronomists. Agronomists observe nature so that they can protect soil. They pay close attention to the different elements that are present in soil. Agronomists want to learn how to improve soil for farmers. They try to find new ways to prevent soil from washing away. Doing experiments helps them accomplish these goals.

Good scientists take notes on everything they discover. They write down their observations. Sometimes those observations lead scientists to ask new questions. With new questions in mind, they design experiments to find the answers.

When scientists design experiments, they must think very clearly. The way they think about problems is often called the scientific method. What is the scientific method? It's a step-by-step way of finding answers to specific questions. The steps don't always follow the same pattern. Sometimes scientists change their minds. The process often works something like this:

Scientific Method

- **Step One:** A scientist gathers the facts and makes observations about one particular thing.
- **Step Two:** The scientist comes up with a question that is not answered by all the observations and facts.
- **Step Three:** The scientist creates a hypothesis. This is a statement of what the scientist thinks is probably the answer to the question.
- **Step Four:** The scientist tests the hypothesis. He or she designs an experiment to see whether the hypothesis is correct. The scientist does the experiment and writes down what happens.
- **Step Five:** The scientist draws a conclusion based on how the experiment turned out. The conclusion might be that the hypothesis is correct. Sometimes, though, the hypothesis is not correct. In that case, the scientist might develop a new hypothesis and another experiment.

In the following experiments, we'll see the scientific method in action. First, we'll gather some facts and observations about soil. For each experiment, we'll also develop a question and a hypothesis. Next, we'll do the experiment to see if our hypothesis is correct. By the end of the experiment, we should know something new about soil. Scientists, are you ready? Then let's get started!

A few words about the soil you'll use for these experiments

To get the best results, use soil that you dig up from your backyard or a spot at your school. But before you dig, get permission from your parents or teacher! Don't use a bag of potting soil from a nursery or gardening center, and don't use soil that contains too much sand or clay. If you are doing these experiments in a classroom and need a lot of soil, you'll probably have luck at the following places:

- The agronomy department at a local college or university
- A local 4-H program
- Your local extension office. This is a government program that does research related to agriculture, which is the study of farming. To find out if there's an office near you, go to *www.csrees.usda.gov/Extension/*.

Experiment #1
What Is Soil Made Of?

← These cabbage plants need soil to grow.

Soil is all around us. We use it to grow trees and flowers, grass and crops. But have you ever wondered what soil is made of? It might seem like every piece of soil is the same, but is it?

If you dig up a chunk of soil and look at it closely, you'll probably notice different colors and textures in the pile. But why does soil look this way? You may be asking yourself the following question: **Is soil made up of different materials?** To answer this question, you might come up with this hypothesis: **Soil *is* made up of different materials.** Ready to see if you're right?

Here's what you'll need:
- 1 cup of soil
- 1 glass jar, with a lid, that can hold at least 3 cups of water
- 1 cup of water

Make sure the lid of your jar will close tightly.

9

Instructions:

1. Place the soil in the jar, and add 1 cup of water. Screw the lid on tightly. Give the jar a few good shakes until the water and soil are completely mixed together.
2. Put the jar on a counter, and let the mixture settle overnight.
3. Observe the mixture the next day. Be sure to write down everything you notice.

This is almost as much fun as making mud pies!

Conclusion:

What was once muddy water probably now looks like something new. Do you see different layers in the jar? What conclusions can you draw from the fact that layers have formed? What makes up the different layers? Are there any small stones? Perhaps some sand? Organic matter such as leaves and grass are also often found in soil. Do you see any organic matter in your jar?

There are usually 3 main materials found in soil: sand, silt, and clay. If you rub sand between your fingers, it feels rough. Silt is smoother and is slippery when it's wet. Wet clay feels sticky. Most soils have all 3 materials, and soil that contains equal amounts of sand, silt, and clay is known as loam. There are many different types of soil with various combinations of materials, but loam is usually a good mixture for growing healthy plants.

When you look at your layers of soil and water, think about this: Sand is the heaviest type of soil, silt is lighter, and clay is the lightest. Which layer in your jar is sand? Which is silt? Which is clay? Did your soil have more sand, silt, or clay in it?

You've probably used a recipe to bake cookies or a cake, but did you know that there are also recipes for creating good soil? Gardeners know that just the right mixture of sand, silt, and clay—and sometimes stones or organic material such as peat moss—can help form the best soil possible.

Experiment #2

Soil Size

← Look closely—can you see the different particles in the soil?

In the first experiment, we learned that soil is made of different materials. If you take a closer look at different types of soil, you'll probably notice that there are also different sizes of soil particles. Particles are very small pieces of material— they're kind of like grains of salt. Just compare the particles in a handful of sand to the particles in a handful of soil from an area where you plant flowers. What are some of the differences you observe between the two? Does one type of soil have bigger particles than the other?

Your observations may have you asking this question: **Does particle size determine how well water passes through the soil?** Think about a hypothesis that focuses on the connection between particle size and water. Here is an example: **Water will flow more quickly through soil that has bigger particles.** Now, let's see if our hypothesis is correct!

Here's what you'll need:

- 1 toothpick
- 2 identical Styrofoam or paper cups, labeled Cup #1 and Cup #2
- 2 small glass jars (The bottom of each cup should fit inside the opening of each jar without falling down into it.)
- 1 cup of sand
- 1 cup of soil
- 2 cups of water

Make sure you have everything you need before you start.

Pour 1 cup of water into each Styrofoam cup.

Cup #1

Cup #2

Instructions:

1. Use the toothpick to poke about 20 holes in the bottom of each of the cups. Make sure the holes are spaced evenly apart.

2. Place a cup in the opening of each jar. Put the sand in Cup #1 and the soil in Cup #2. Pour 1 cup of water into the sand and 1 cup of water into the soil.

3. Look at your jars after 1 minute. Write down what you see. Is there liquid in either jar? How about after 5 minutes?

Conclusion:

Did we prove our hypothesis? Keep in mind that there is little space between very small soil particles. This makes it harder for water to flow through. Remember that the particles in sandy soil are larger, and there are usually larger spaces between larger particles. This allows water to pass through the soil more quickly.

So, if you lived somewhere with sandy soil, would you have to water your plants more or less often than if you were in an area with less sandy soil? What could you do to sandy soil if you wanted to stop the water from flowing through it too quickly? One possibility would be to add organic matter such as compost or peat moss. These materials act like sponges and help keep the water from draining too fast.

Adding organic matter to soil makes it better for growing plants.

Experiment #3

Stop It!

← Coffee filters keep coffee grounds out of brewed coffee.

Have you ever watched someone put a paper filter in a coffeemaker? The filter holds ground coffee but allows water to pass through. This means that no one has to worry about drinking crunchy coffee!

In our last experiment, we saw that water moved more slowly when it flowed through soil with smaller particles. Let's take that idea a step further by asking the following question: **Can soil**

with smaller particles actually block something and act as a natural filter? What do you think the answer is? Let's try the following hypothesis: **Soil with smaller or finer particles *can* act as a natural filter.** Experiment #3 will determine whether we are correct!

Here's what you'll need:
- 1 toothpick
- 1 Styrofoam or paper cup
- 1 small glass jar (The bottom of the cup should fit inside the opening of the jar without falling down into it.)
- 1 cup of soil (Pick a soil that doesn't feel too gritty. Gritty soil usually has more sand in it and allows liquid to pass through more quickly.)
- 1½ cups of a red drink (such as Kool-Aid)
- 1 clear drinking glass

Gather the items you need.

Instructions:

1. Use the toothpick to poke about 20 evenly spaced holes into the bottom of the cup.
2. Place the cup in the top of the jar, and put the soil in it.
3. Pour 1 cup of the red drink into the soil. Pour the remaining ½ cup of the drink into the glass. Wait about 30 to 60 minutes. Then check to see if any liquid has passed through the soil and flowed into the jar. If it hasn't, you might need to wait a bit longer.
4. Once you do have liquid in the jar, compare it to the liquid in the glass. Write down your observations. Are the liquids the same color? Is the liquid that passed through the soil a lighter color?

Be careful not to spill the liquid!

Conclusion:

What can you conclude based on the color of the liquid that flowed through the soil? The red color represents substances that may be present in water. Remember that smaller or finer soil particles are closer to one another than larger soil particles. This causes water to flow more slowly through the soil. As a result, substances can get trapped more easily than they would in soil with larger particles. So, you have learned that water that passes through soil with smaller or finer particles is filtered.

Did you know that soil can be used to help filter dirty water? Septic tanks are watertight boxes that hold wastewater from your house. These tanks are used in areas that don't have a sewer pipe system. While solid waste remains in the tank, some dirty liquids pass through a pipe into the soil around it. The soil works like a filter and traps much of the filthy material that is present in the water.

Experiment #4
Don't Wash It Away

Soil filters water, but what does water do to soil? ⟶

Our third experiment proved that soil can act as a water filter. But here's another important question: **How does water affect different kinds of soil?** Think about it. Have you ever watered a garden? Did the rushing water from the hose cause the soil to change or move around? Keep your experiences in mind as you come up with a hypothesis about how water affects various kinds of soil. Here is a possibility: **Water causes different types of soil to erode or wash away.** Want to do a little scientific work to see if you're right?

Here's what you'll need:

- At least 4 cups of soil
- A large pan, such as a 9 x 13 baking pan or something similar. Just be sure that the pan has sides that are at least 1.5 inches (3.8 centimeters) high.
- A small plastic container
- Water
- Some rocks and stones
- 2 cups of peat or leaves that are ripped into small pieces

Don't forget your notebook to record what you observe!

Instructions:

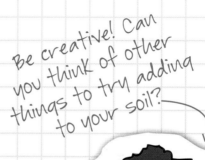

1. Place the soil in the pan. Use the plastic container to add small amounts of water to the soil, until it's moist enough to shape into a hill.

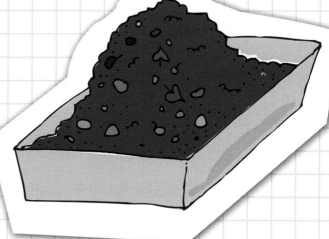

Be creative! Can you think of other things to try adding to your soil?

2. Divide your hill into 3 vertical sections. Put rocks and stones on part of your hill. Add the leaves or peat to another section. Make sure that you actually push these materials into the soil, instead of simply laying them on top of it. Leave the last part of the hill bare.

3. Refill your container with water, and slowly pour it down the top of the hill. Make sure to pour the water over the different sides of the hill where you have placed different materials.

4. Observe what happens as water flows over each side of the hill. Don't forget to write down everything you notice!

Conclusion:

What happened to the part of the hill that's covered with rocks and stones? What happened to the section of the hill that has leaves or peat? What happened to the side of the hill that is bare soil?

Did you get different results in different areas? Did more soil wash away in one section than another? What conclusions can you make based on what you observed? How could you use this information to stop the soil from washing away on a real hill?

Have you ever seen a hilly area where there are no grasses or other plants? What do you think would happen to the soil there if a big rainstorm came along?

Water is not the only thing that can cause soil erosion. Wind can, too. During the 1930s, much of the land in the south-central United States became known as the Dust Bowl during a terrible dry period called a drought. The strong prairie grasses that didn't need much water had been plowed under to grow wheat. But no rain meant no wheat would grow. So when strong winds blew, there was nothing to keep the dry soil from eroding. The blowing soil created so much dust that it even buried some local houses!

Experiment #5

Should You Feed Your Soil?

← You need good food. Does soil need food, too?

Have you ever heard the phrase "You are what you eat"? It means that it's important to eat nourishing foods if you want to have a healthy body. Connect this saying to soil by asking the following question: **Are certain materials needed to keep soil healthy?**

Since much of the food that we eat every day is grown in the earth, this is an interesting topic. Of course, scientists don't always have a single hypothesis when it comes to important issues. Why not consider a few for our final experiment? Pick whichever hypothesis you believe is correct:

Hypothesis #1: Certain materials in soil help make it more fertile.

Hypothesis #2: The different materials in soil have no effect on how fertile the soil is.

Are you ready to find out if the hypothesis you chose was correct?

What do carrots need to grow big and healthy?

Here's what you'll need:

- 1 cup of sand
- 1 cup of plain soil
- 1 cup of soil mixed with any of the following materials: peat, grass clippings, straw, wood chips, or sawdust
- 3 Styrofoam or paper cups, labeled Cup #1, Cup #2, and Cup #3
- 1 package of radish seeds
- Water
- A tablespoon

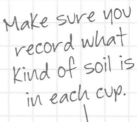

Make sure you record what kind of soil is in each cup.

Instructions:

1. Put the sand in Cup #1, the plain soil in Cup #2, and the soil that you've "fed" with other materials into Cup #3.

2. Follow the instructions on your package of radish seeds, and plant 4 or 5 seeds in each cup. (Be sure to put the exact same number of seeds in every cup, and write down how many seeds you planted.)
3. Lightly water each cup, and place it in a warm, sunny spot such as a windowsill. The cups should be in the same area, so that they're all getting the same amount of heat and light.

4. Check your cups every day. If the soil is dry, add water until it appears damp. Use a tablespoon to measure how much water you add. Keep track of how many tablespoons you need to water your plants. Write down the amounts.

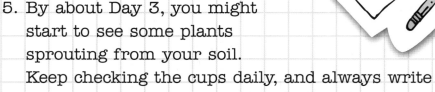

5. By about Day 3, you might start to see some plants sprouting from your soil. Keep checking the cups daily, and always write down your observations. Which type of soil caused the seeds to sprout first? Second? Last?

6. Continue watering your plants whenever the soil seems dry. Do you have to water some plants more often than others? Which type of soil seems to dry out the fastest?

Conclusion:

How many of your seeds sprouted? Did more plants grow in one type of soil than another? Do the plants in one type of soil look healthier than the plants in another? Why do you think this is? What can you conclude about how the different materials in soil affect plant growth?

Do It Yourself!

← Scientists share their findings with one another.

Now you know a lot more about soil than when you started these experiments. Does that mean you have all the answers? Probably not. In fact, you may have more questions than when you started.

Maybe you are wondering which kind of soil is best for growing plants in containers. Or which soil you should use to grow flowers.

Write down all of your questions. Then pick one you'd like answered. Come up with a hypothesis. Design an experiment to test your hypothesis. You'll need to gather your materials, do the experiment, write down your observations, and draw a conclusion. You are well on your way to becoming a top-notch scientist!

Do you look at soil differently after all the experiments you've completed? Are you starting to see that it's more than "just dirt"? Soil is a big part of your life, and you don't even have to get dirty to enjoy it! So the next time you plant a seed, build a sand castle, or enjoy some flowers, remember everything you know about soil—and science!

You can always build on what you learn. Keep experimenting!

GLOSSARY

agronomists (uh-GRAH-nuh-mistss) scientists who study how to care for farmland and grow crops

conclusion (kuhn-KLOO-zhuhn) a final decision, thought, or opinion

erode (i-RODE) to cause something to wear away over time

hypothesis (hy-POTH-uh-sihss) a logical guess about what will happen in an experiment

loam (LOHM) a rich soil that's made of equal amounts of sand, clay, and silt

method (METH-uhd) a way of doing something

observations (ob-zur-VAY-shuhnz) things that are seen or noticed with one's senses

organic matter (or-GAN-ick MAT-ur) rotting plants that eventually break down to become soil

textures (TEKS-churz) the feel of different materials or substances

FOR MORE INFORMATION

BOOKS

Faulkner, Rebecca. *Soil*. Chicago: Raintree, 2007.

Gardner, Robert, and Tom LaBaff (illustrator). *Super Science Projects about Earth's Soil and Water*. Berkeley Heights, NJ: Enslow Publishers, 2008.

Walker, Sally M. *Soil*. Minneapolis: Lerner Publications Company, 2007.

WEB SITES

42eXplore—The Topic: Soils

42explore.com/dirt.htm

Everything you ever wanted to know about soil, plus lots of interesting science experiments

HowStuffWorks—Science Projects for Kids: Soil Experiments

home.howstuffworks.com/science-projects-for-kids-soil-experiments.htm

Ideas for easy experiments with soil that kids can do at home

West Texas A&M University—K–12 Teaching Resources and Activities (by Dr. Dirt)

www.wtamu.edu/~crobinson/DrDirt.htm

Further information about soil, and additional experiments kids can do with it

INDEX

About the Author →

Vicky Franchino decided to tackle soil experiments because she knew she could rely on her good friend, Emmett Schulte, a retired agronomy professor, for help. Franchino lives in Madison, Wisconsin, with her husband and three daughters. She now knows that soil is what you grow plants in; dirt is what your mom makes you wash off your hands before dinner.